# Dance Th

## *Moving With Your Creativity...*

Janaea Rose Lyn

&

Laura Higgins Palmer

**Dance This Notebook!**
**Moving With Your Creativity...**

© 2012 by Janaea Rose Lyn and Laura Higgins Palmer

Printed in the United States of America

Library of Congress Control Number: 2012950076

**ISBN: 978-0-692-01824-8**

Printed by CreateSpace

Available from Amazon.com, CreateSpace.com,
VillageBooks.com and other retail outlets

For artwork and merchandising permission contact
LHP@StudioLHP.com

This personal journal was
designed collaboratively by a dancer and an artist
as an
*imaginative space*
within which to
record your creativity.


May you enjoy using it
as much as we enjoyed making it.

*Happy Dancing!*

*- Janaea and Laura*

Dedication:

All great accomplishments began with a leap of faith,

Take yours...

Spinning,

    Spinning,

        Spinning,

           without ending or beginning...

    Children understand why.

A sacred space invites imagination to visit.

How to begin? Simply start and then continue...!

Let your Intention guide you like the North Star

through the great Open space of possibilities

to arrive surely

at your creative destination.

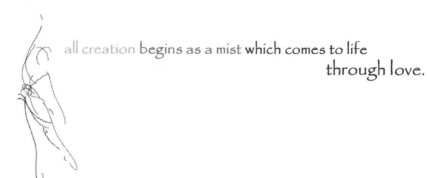

all creation begins as a mist which comes to life
through love.

You are never alone,

your ancestors are always

dancing with you.

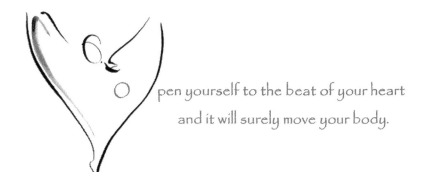 pen yourself to the beat of your heart
and it will surely move your body.

notes...

We are always circling back to who we were. we than more become to order in

Attitude is a state of mind first.

Leave the earth and see a new perspective.

Creation, Reflection, Expression

the Muses travel together.

One by one our steps are made.

...our limbs are free to turn towards the Sky.

When our Roots are deep and solid ...

The flame of creation can never be extinguished.

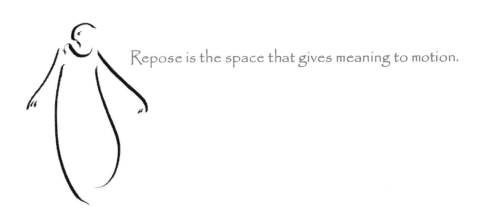

Repose is the space that gives meaning to motion.

Questions, like movements,

lead to more and better ones...

Blend when you must, but don't lose yourself.

Toss something wonderful out every time you create

and something even better will arrive.

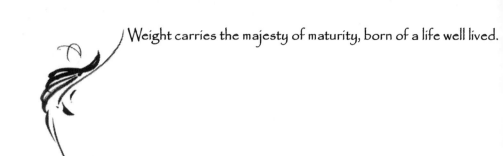

Weight carries the majesty of maturity, born of a life well lived.

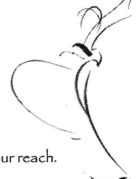

The fullness of life is within your reach.

Reach back, call the others to join you,

they are waiting to be invited along...

If
you
always
bend
you
will
never
Break.

Every gesture undulates

with the promise of another to come.

We are all connected in one family tree.

Become one with the wind.

Shadows remind us there is always another perspective.

-We all need support sometimes.

Trust what you feel but cannot see.

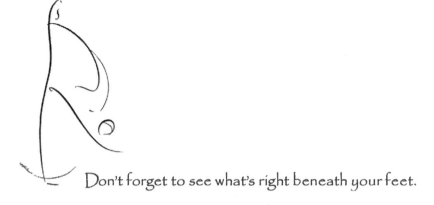

Don't forget to see what's right beneath your feet.

Friends complement each other.

notes...

When we collaborate

we become more                                    than ourselves.

we become Community.

.

We all have wings but some of us

have forgotten to use them.

Listen and you will hear the rhythm ⌒⟍ of the spheres.

In stillness grows the seed from which the tree is born.

Life is a balancing act. Stay steady.

 Dance your way through life...

. . . and live your way through dance.

You are

your own

Masterpiece!

## Acknowledgments:

Special Thanks to Tim McAlee, Doug & Ada Palmer, Dianne Hunt, Rebecca Powers, Lisa O'Hara, Karen Berdoulay, Eleni Theodaris, Heather Kern and everyone who helped bring  Dance This Notebook to life.

## About the Authors:

**Janaea Rose Lyn** is a dance artist, educator and writer with a particular focus on creating and facilitating collaborative projects. She currently lives in Phoenix, Arizona and is on the faculty of Estrella Mountain Community College. Additionally, Janaea is active as a third-generation Isadora Duncan Dancer and Historian, and is a contributing writer for Choreoclinic.com and DanceAdvantage.net.

Previously, she was Assistant Professor of Dance at Cecil College in Maryland and Founding Artistic Director of Dance Matrix and Convergence Dancers & Musicians.

**www.janaearoselyn.com  or  janaealyn@gmail.com**

**Laura Higgins Palmer** has been working directly with dancers and choreographers for more than two decades. From countless volumes of her drawings Laura creates finished paintings based on improvisations, observations, characters, and theatrical productions.  Laura's work has been exhibited internationally and she has taught drawing, painting, design, figure and anatomy to students from elementary school through college and beyond.

**www.StudioLHP.com  or  www.Drawn2Dance.com**

Made in the USA
San Bernardino, CA
20 November 2015